EMMANUEL JOSEPH

The Fabric of Responsibility, Ecology, Ethics, and the Future of Fashion

Copyright © 2025 by Emmanuel Joseph

All rights reserved. No part of this publication may be reproduced, stored or transmitted in any form or by any means, electronic, mechanical, photocopying, recording, scanning, or otherwise without written permission from the publisher. It is illegal to copy this book, post it to a website, or distribute it by any other means without permission.

First edition

This book was professionally typeset on Reedsy. Find out more at reedsy.com

Contents

1	Chapter 1: The Interwoven Tapestry of Ecology and Fashion	1
2	Chapter 2: Unraveling the Threads of Fast Fashion	3
3	Chapter 3: The Environmental Cost of Textile Production	5
4	Chapter 4: Ethical Sourcing and Fair Trade in Fashion	7
5	Chapter 5: The Role of Technology in Sustainable Fashion	9
6	Chapter 6: The Power of Consumer Choice	11
7	Chapter 7: The Impact of Fashion on Biodiversity	13
8	Chapter 8: Fashion as a Tool for Social Change	15
9	Chapter 9: Fashion's Influence on Identity and Culture	17
10	Chapter 10: The Future of Sustainable Fashion	19
11	Chapter 11: The Role of Policy and Legislation in...	21
12	Chapter 12: The Intersection of Fashion and Climate Change	23
13	Chapter 13: The Role of Innovation in Sustainable Fashion	25
14	Chapter 14: The Importance of Education and Awareness in...	27
15	Chapter 15: The Role of Creativity and Innovation in...	29
16	Chapter 16: The Intersection of Fashion and Technology	31
17	Chapter 17: The Collective Responsibility of Fashion	33

1

Chapter 1: The Interwoven Tapestry of Ecology and Fashion

Fashion, often synonymous with fleeting trends and superficial glamour, holds a deeper, complex interconnection with the environment. Beneath the glitz and fabric lies a monumental ecological footprint that has transformed our rivers, lands, and even the air we breathe. As the industry propels forward, the question arises: at what cost to our planet? Unbeknownst to many, each piece of clothing tells a story of water usage, chemical application, and waste production. The fashion industry is the second-largest polluter globally, after oil, leading to pressing environmental concerns. The synthetic fibers, which make up about 60% of our clothing, release microplastics into the oceans, disrupting marine ecosystems. Additionally, the vast amounts of water required for cotton production have led to the depletion of major water bodies, exacerbating the world's water scarcity issues.

As consumers, the clothes we choose reflect our values and responsibility toward the planet. The fast fashion trend, characterized by mass production and rapid disposal, mirrors our unsustainable consumption patterns. Every discarded garment adds to the mounting landfills, which are already straining under the pressure of accumulated waste. This relentless cycle of production and disposal not only squanders valuable resources but also poses severe environmental hazards. The harsh dyes and chemicals used in textile manufacturing often seep into soil and waterways, causing contamination that affects both wildlife and human health. By understanding the ecological impact of fashion, we can begin to make more informed decisions that align with a sustainable future.

However, a shift is underway. Brands and consumers alike are starting to recognize the urgent need for sustainable practices within the industry. Innovations in textile recycling, the development of eco-friendly fabrics, and an emphasis on ethical production methods are promising signs of change. Companies are beginning to adopt circular economy principles, where materials are continuously repurposed rather than discarded. This paradigm shift emphasizes reducing waste, reusing resources, and recycling materials, thereby minimizing the environmental footprint. Additionally, transparency in supply chains is becoming a focal point, allowing consumers to trace the origins of their clothing and make more conscious purchasing decisions. The collaboration between fashion and environmental advocacy is fostering a new narrative where style coexists harmoniously with sustainability.

The journey toward a responsible fashion industry requires collective effort and systemic change. It begins with reimagining our relationship with clothing—viewing garments not as disposable commodities but as valuable assets worthy of care and longevity. This paradigm shift challenges both producers and consumers to adopt ethical practices and sustainable habits. By supporting brands that prioritize eco-conscious practices and by embracing a mindful approach to fashion, we can drive the industry toward a future where beauty and ethics are seamlessly woven together. Together, we have the power to transform the fabric of fashion into one that respects and protects our planet.

2

Chapter 2: Unraveling the Threads of Fast Fashion

The allure of fast fashion lies in its affordability and accessibility, allowing consumers to indulge in the latest trends without breaking the bank. However, this rapid turnover of styles comes with hidden costs that extend far beyond the price tags. Fast fashion relies on a model of mass production, where garments are designed, manufactured, and delivered to stores in a matter of weeks. This accelerated pace often leads to compromised quality and craftsmanship, resulting in clothing that is meant to be worn a few times before being discarded. The environmental impact of this throwaway culture is staggering, with millions of tons of textile waste ending up in landfills each year. Furthermore, the energy consumption and greenhouse gas emissions associated with fast fashion production contribute significantly to climate change.

The social implications of fast fashion are equally concerning. The demand for cheap, fast-produced clothing often drives manufacturers to cut corners, leading to exploitative labor practices. Workers in developing countries are subjected to long hours, unsafe working conditions, and meager wages, all in the name of keeping prices low for consumers. These labor abuses highlight the ethical responsibility that brands and consumers share in addressing the human cost of fashion. By raising awareness of these issues and advocating for fair labor practices, we can begin to shift the industry toward a more ethical and sustainable model.

Consumers play a crucial role in driving change within the fast fashion industry. By making conscious choices, such as opting for quality over quantity and supporting brands with transparent and ethical practices, we can reduce the demand for fast fashion. Additionally, embracing a minimalist wardrobe and investing in timeless, durable pieces can help curb the cycle of overconsumption. Sustainable fashion also encourages the practice of upcycling and repurposing garments, giving new life to old clothes and reducing waste. By rethinking our approach to fashion, we can contribute to a more sustainable and ethical industry.

The movement toward slow fashion offers a promising alternative to the fast fashion paradigm. Slow fashion emphasizes quality, craftsmanship, and sustainability, prioritizing the well-being of both people and the planet. This approach encourages consumers to build a thoughtful wardrobe with pieces that are made to last, rather than succumbing to fleeting trends. Brands that embrace slow fashion often focus on sustainable materials, ethical production methods, and transparent supply chains. By supporting these brands and adopting a mindful approach to fashion, we can collectively drive the industry toward a future that values responsibility and sustainability.

3

Chapter 3: The Environmental Cost of Textile Production

Textile production, the backbone of the fashion industry, has a profound impact on the environment. The journey from raw materials to finished garments involves numerous stages, each with its own set of environmental challenges. From the cultivation of cotton to the manufacturing of synthetic fibers, the process consumes vast amounts of water, energy, and chemicals. For instance, cotton, one of the most widely used natural fibers, requires significant water resources for irrigation. The excessive use of water in cotton farming has led to the depletion of major water bodies, such as the Aral Sea, and has exacerbated water scarcity in many regions. Additionally, the use of pesticides and fertilizers in cotton cultivation contributes to soil degradation and water pollution.

Synthetic fibers, such as polyester and nylon, are derived from petroleum, a non-renewable resource. The production of these fibers involves energy-intensive processes and generates greenhouse gas emissions, contributing to global warming. Furthermore, synthetic fibers release microplastics when washed, which eventually make their way into oceans and pose a threat to marine life. The dyeing and finishing processes in textile manufacturing also have significant environmental impacts. The use of toxic chemicals in dyes and treatments can lead to water contamination, affecting both aquatic ecosystems and human health. The discharge of untreated wastewater from textile factories into rivers and streams is a common practice in many countries, further exacerbating pollution.

To mitigate the environmental impact of textile production, the industry must adopt sustainable practices and technologies. Innovations in eco-friendly fabrics, such as organic cotton, hemp, and recycled materials, offer promising alternatives to conventional textiles. These materials require fewer resources and have a lower environmental footprint. Additionally, advancements in dyeing technologies, such as waterless dyeing and the use of natural dyes, can significantly reduce water consumption and chemical usage. Implementing cleaner production methods and investing in wastewater treatment systems can also help minimize pollution.

The concept of a circular economy presents a holistic approach to addressing the environmental challenges of textile production. In a circular economy, materials are kept in use for as long as possible, through recycling, upcycling, and repurposing. This approach reduces waste and conserves resources, creating a closed-loop system that mimics natural processes. By embracing circular economy principles, the fashion industry can transition toward a more sustainable model that values resource efficiency and environmental stewardship.

4

Chapter 4: Ethical Sourcing and Fair Trade in Fashion

Ethical sourcing and fair trade are cornerstones of a responsible fashion industry. Ethical sourcing refers to the practice of procuring materials and products in a manner that respects human rights, environmental sustainability, and social responsibility. Fair trade, on the other hand, focuses on creating equitable trading relationships that provide fair wages and safe working conditions for producers in developing countries. Both concepts are integral to building a fashion industry that prioritizes ethics and sustainability over profit.

The journey of a garment often begins with the sourcing of raw materials, such as cotton, wool, or synthetic fibers. Ethical sourcing ensures that these materials are obtained in ways that do not exploit workers or harm the environment. For example, organic cotton is grown without the use of harmful pesticides and fertilizers, promoting soil health and reducing water pollution. Similarly, ethical wool production prioritizes animal welfare and sustainable land management practices. By choosing materials that are sustainably sourced, brands can reduce their environmental footprint and support communities that depend on these resources for their livelihoods.

Fair trade practices extend beyond material sourcing to encompass the entire supply chain, from production to distribution. Fair trade certification ensures that workers receive fair wages, work in safe conditions, and have access to social benefits such as healthcare and education. This certification also promotes community development by investing in local infrastructure and education projects. By supporting fair trade, consumers can contribute to the well-being of workers and their communities, fostering a more equitable and just fashion industry.

Transparency is a key aspect of ethical sourcing and fair trade. Brands that prioritize transparency provide detailed information about their supply chains, allowing consumers to trace the origins of their garments. This transparency builds trust and accountability, enabling consumers to make informed choices that align with their values. Furthermore, brands that are committed to ethical sourcing often engage in third-party audits and certifications to ensure compliance with social and environmental standards.

The rise of conscious consumerism is driving demand for ethically sourced and fair trade products. Consumers are increasingly seeking out brands that prioritize sustainability and social responsibility. This shift in consumer behavior is encouraging brands to adopt ethical practices and promote their commitments to fair trade. By making conscious choices and supporting ethical brands, consumers can drive positive change within the fashion industry, creating a future where fashion is synonymous with fairness and sustainability.

5

Chapter 5: The Role of Technology in Sustainable Fashion

The integration of technology in the fashion industry is revolutionizing the way garments are designed, produced, and consumed. Innovative technologies are driving sustainability by reducing waste, conserving resources, and enhancing the overall efficiency of the fashion supply chain. From 3D printing to blockchain, these advancements are paving the way for a more eco-conscious future in fashion.

3D printing technology, for instance, offers the potential to create customized garments with minimal material waste. By precisely controlling the amount of fabric used, 3D printing reduces the need for excess inventory and minimizes production waste. Additionally, this technology allows for on-demand manufacturing, eliminating the need for mass production and overstocking. The ability to produce garments locally also reduces the carbon footprint associated with transportation and logistics.

Blockchain technology is another groundbreaking innovation that enhances transparency and traceability in the fashion supply chain. By providing a decentralized and tamper-proof ledger, blockchain enables brands to track the journey of a garment from raw material to finished product. This transparency ensures that ethical and sustainable practices are upheld at every stage of production. Consumers can access detailed information about the origins of their clothing, empowering them to make informed purchasing decisions. Blockchain also facilitates the authentication of products, reducing the prevalence of counterfeit goods in the market.

Artificial intelligence (AI) and machine learning are transforming the way fashion companies predict trends and manage inventory. By analyzing vast amounts of data, AI algorithms can forecast consumer preferences and optimize production schedules, reducing waste and overproduction. Furthermore, AI-powered tools can assist in designing garments that are both stylish and sustainable, taking into account factors such as material choice, production methods, and end-of-life considerations. These technologies are enabling fashion brands to adopt more efficient and sustainable practices, ultimately contributing to a circular economy.

The rise of digital fashion and virtual try-ons is also making a significant impact on sustainability. Virtual fashion platforms allow consumers to experiment with different styles and outfits without physically purchasing the items. This reduces the demand for fast fashion and encourages a more mindful approach to clothing consumption. Virtual try-ons, powered by augmented reality (AR), enable consumers to visualize how garments will look and fit, reducing the likelihood of returns and associated environmental costs. By leveraging these technologies, the fashion industry can promote sustainability while enhancing the consumer experience.

6

Chapter 6: The Power of Consumer Choice

Consumers hold immense power in shaping the future of fashion through their purchasing decisions and consumption habits. The choices we make as consumers can either perpetuate harmful practices or drive positive change within the industry. By prioritizing sustainability and ethics in our fashion choices, we can collectively contribute to a more responsible and eco-friendly fashion landscape.

One of the most effective ways consumers can support sustainable fashion is by choosing quality over quantity. Investing in well-made, durable garments that are designed to last not only reduces waste but also encourages brands to prioritize craftsmanship and sustainability. By building a timeless wardrobe with versatile pieces, consumers can minimize the need for frequent purchases and reduce their overall environmental footprint. Additionally, opting for secondhand and vintage clothing extends the lifespan of garments and promotes a circular economy.

Supporting brands that prioritize ethical and sustainable practices is another powerful way consumers can drive change. Many fashion brands are adopting eco-friendly materials, transparent supply chains, and fair labor practices. By researching and supporting these brands, consumers can encourage the industry to move toward more responsible and sustainable practices. Certifications such as Fair Trade, GOTS (Global Organic Textile Standard), and B Corp provide valuable information about a brand's commitment to sustainability and ethics.

Practicing mindful consumption is key to reducing the environmental impact of fashion. This involves being conscious of our purchasing habits and considering the true cost of our clothing choices. Before making a purchase, consumers can ask themselves questions such as: Do I really need this item? How often will I wear it? Is it made from sustainable materials? By adopting a thoughtful approach to fashion, consumers can avoid impulse buys and make more intentional choices that align with their values.

Embracing sustainable fashion also involves taking care of the garments we already own. Proper maintenance, such as washing clothes in cold water, air-drying, and repairing instead of discarding, can significantly extend the lifespan of clothing. Consumers can also explore creative ways to upcycle and repurpose old garments, giving them a new lease on life and reducing waste. By nurturing a culture of care and longevity, we can foster a more sustainable and responsible approach to fashion consumption.

7

Chapter 7: The Impact of Fashion on Biodiversity

The fashion industry has far-reaching effects on biodiversity, affecting ecosystems and wildlife in various ways. The cultivation of raw materials, such as cotton and wool, often involves the use of pesticides, herbicides, and fertilizers, which can harm plant and animal species. Monoculture farming practices, where a single crop is grown extensively, reduce biodiversity and disrupt natural habitats. For instance, large-scale cotton farming has led to the decline of native plant species and the displacement of wildlife in many regions.

The production of synthetic fibers, such as polyester and nylon, also poses significant threats to biodiversity. These fibers are derived from petrochemicals and contribute to the depletion of fossil fuels. The manufacturing process releases harmful chemicals into the environment, affecting soil, water, and air quality. Additionally, the microplastics shed by synthetic fibers during washing end up in oceans, posing a threat to marine life. These microplastics are ingested by fish and other marine organisms, causing harm to their health and entering the food chain.

The fashion industry's reliance on exotic animal materials, such as fur, leather, and feathers, has further implications for biodiversity. The demand for these materials drives the hunting and farming of animals, often under inhumane conditions. This not only raises ethical concerns but also disrupts natural ecosystems and contributes to the decline of endangered species. For example, the fur trade has led to the endangerment of species such as the Canadian lynx and the sea otter. The illegal wildlife trade, fueled by the demand for exotic animal materials, exacerbates the loss of biodiversity and threatens the survival of many species.

To mitigate the impact of fashion on biodiversity, the industry must adopt more sustainable and ethical practices. This includes sourcing materials from sustainable and regenerative agricultural practices that prioritize biodiversity and ecosystem health. For instance, organic cotton farming promotes soil health and reduces the use of harmful chemicals, benefiting both biodiversity and the environment. Additionally, the development of eco-friendly alternatives to animal materials, such as lab-grown leather and plant-based fabrics, can reduce the demand for exotic animal products and protect wildlife.

Conservation efforts and collaboration with environmental organizations are also crucial in addressing the impact of fashion on biodiversity. Brands can support initiatives that protect natural habitats, restore ecosystems, and promote biodiversity conservation. By raising awareness and advocating for sustainable practices, the fashion industry can contribute to the preservation of our planet's rich biodiversity and ensure a thriving future for all species.

8

Chapter 8: Fashion as a Tool for Social Change

Fashion has the power to influence societal values and drive social change. Throughout history, clothing and style have been used as symbols of identity, culture, and resistance. From the suffragette movement to the civil rights era, fashion has played a pivotal role in shaping social movements and advocating for change. In contemporary times, the fashion industry continues to be a platform for addressing social issues and promoting inclusivity, diversity, and equality.

The rise of ethical fashion has brought attention to the social and environmental impact of clothing production. By prioritizing fair labor practices, sustainable materials, and transparent supply chains, ethical fashion brands are challenging the conventional norms of the industry. These brands advocate for the rights and well-being of workers, often partnering with artisans and communities to create products that reflect their cultural heritage. By supporting ethical fashion, consumers can contribute to positive social change and empower marginalized communities.

Fashion activism is another powerful tool for raising awareness and advocating for social issues. Designers, influencers, and consumers are using fashion as a means of expression and protest. For instance, the "Fashion Revolution" movement encourages consumers to ask brands, "Who made my clothes?" This campaign highlights the importance of transparency and accountability in the fashion industry, urging brands to disclose information about their supply chains and labor practices. Similarly, initiatives like "Black Lives Matter" and "Me Too" have used fashion as a platform to amplify their messages and promote social justice.

Inclusivity and diversity are central to the social change movement within fashion. The industry is increasingly recognizing the importance of representation and embracing diverse voices and perspectives. This includes celebrating different body types, ethnicities, genders, and abilities in fashion campaigns and runway shows. By promoting inclusivity, the fashion industry can challenge stereotypes and foster a more inclusive and equitable society.

Fashion education also plays a crucial role in driving social change. By incorporating sustainability, ethics, and social responsibility into fashion curricula, educational institutions can equip the next generation of designers and industry professionals with the knowledge and skills to create positive change. Initiatives such as workshops, internships, and collaborations with ethical brands provide students with hands-on experience in sustainable fashion practices. By fostering a culture of innovation and social consciousness, fashion education can inspire future leaders to drive the industry toward a more responsible and inclusive future.

9

Chapter 9: Fashion's Influence on Identity and Culture

Fashion has long been a powerful medium for expressing identity and culture. Clothing choices often reflect personal values, beliefs, and social affiliations. Throughout history, different styles and garments have been used to signify cultural heritage, social status, and group identity. For instance, traditional clothing such as kimonos, saris, and kilts carry deep cultural significance and tell stories of ancestral traditions and customs. In contemporary times, fashion continues to be a form of self-expression, allowing individuals to communicate their unique personalities and perspectives.

The influence of fashion on identity is particularly evident in subcultures and social movements. Subcultures such as punk, goth, and hip-hop have used fashion as a way to challenge mainstream norms and assert their distinct identities. The styles associated with these subcultures often carry symbolic meanings and reflect the values and attitudes of their members. For example, the punk movement in the 1970s embraced an anti-establishment ethos, using fashion as a form of rebellion against societal conventions. Similarly, the hip-hop culture has used fashion to celebrate creativity, individuality, and empowerment.

Fashion also plays a significant role in shaping cultural perceptions and trends. Influential designers and fashion houses often set the tone for what is considered fashionable and desirable. Runway shows, fashion magazines, and social media platforms serve as powerful channels for disseminating fashion trends and influencing consumer behavior. The impact of fashion on culture is further amplified by celebrities and influencers who use their platforms to showcase their personal style and endorse brands. This interplay between fashion and culture creates a dynamic and ever-evolving landscape where trends and identities are constantly being redefined.

However, the globalization of fashion has also raised concerns about cultural appropriation and the commodification of cultural symbols. When elements of a culture are used out of context or without understanding and respect, it can lead to misrepresentation and exploitation. For instance, the use of indigenous patterns and designs by fashion brands without proper acknowledgment or compensation has sparked debates about cultural sensitivity and respect. To address these issues, the fashion industry must prioritize ethical practices and collaborate with cultural communities to ensure that their heritage is honored and preserved.

10

Chapter 10: The Future of Sustainable Fashion

The future of fashion lies in sustainability and innovation. As the industry grapples with its environmental and social impacts, a new wave of forward-thinking designers, brands, and consumers are driving the movement toward a more responsible and sustainable future. This transformation is characterized by a commitment to ethical practices, eco-friendly materials, and circular economy principles.

One of the key trends shaping the future of sustainable fashion is the adoption of regenerative agriculture. Unlike conventional farming practices that deplete soil and harm ecosystems, regenerative agriculture focuses on restoring soil health, enhancing biodiversity, and sequestering carbon. By sourcing materials from regenerative farms, fashion brands can contribute to the regeneration of ecosystems and reduce their environmental footprint. This approach not only benefits the environment but also supports the livelihoods of farmers and rural communities.

The rise of biodesign and biofabrication is another exciting development in sustainable fashion. Scientists and designers are exploring the potential of living organisms, such as bacteria and fungi, to create biodegradable and eco-friendly materials. For example, mycelium, the root structure of fungi, can be used to produce leather-like materials that are durable and sustainable.

Similarly, microbial fermentation processes can generate bio-based fibers that serve as alternatives to traditional textiles. These innovations hold the promise of revolutionizing the fashion industry by offering materials that are both sustainable and versatile.

The concept of circular fashion is gaining traction as a holistic solution to the industry's waste problem. Circular fashion emphasizes the reuse, recycling, and repurposing of materials, creating a closed-loop system that mimics natural processes. Brands are adopting circular practices by designing products with longevity in mind, offering repair and take-back programs, and using recycled materials in their collections. This shift toward circularity not only reduces waste but also conserves resources and minimizes the environmental impact of fashion production.

Consumer engagement and education are essential to the success of sustainable fashion. By raising awareness about the environmental and social implications of fashion, brands can empower consumers to make informed choices. Initiatives such as sustainability labels, certification programs, and educational campaigns play a crucial role in promoting transparency and accountability within the industry. As consumers become more conscious of their purchasing decisions, they can drive demand for sustainable products and support brands that prioritize ethics and sustainability.

11

Chapter 11: The Role of Policy and Legislation in Sustainable Fashion

Government policies and legislation play a vital role in shaping the fashion industry's approach to sustainability. By implementing regulations and incentives, policymakers can drive positive change and hold brands accountable for their environmental and social impacts. The fashion industry's transition to sustainability requires collaboration between governments, industry stakeholders, and consumers to create a regulatory framework that promotes ethical practices and environmental stewardship.

One of the key areas where policy intervention is needed is in addressing the environmental impact of textile production. Regulations that limit the use of harmful chemicals, promote water conservation, and encourage the adoption of clean technologies can significantly reduce the industry's environmental footprint. For instance, the European Union's REACH regulation aims to protect human health and the environment by restricting the use of hazardous chemicals in products, including textiles. By setting clear standards and enforcing compliance, governments can ensure that fashion brands prioritize sustainable practices in their production processes.

Extended Producer Responsibility (EPR) is another policy approach that can drive sustainability in fashion. EPR places the responsibility for the entire lifecycle of a product, including its disposal, on the manufacturer. This encourages brands to design products with longevity and recyclability in mind, reducing waste and promoting a circular economy. EPR schemes can also include take-back programs, where consumers can return used garments to brands for recycling or repurposing. By holding producers accountable for the end-of-life management of their products, EPR policies can incentivize sustainable design and reduce the burden on landfills.

Trade policies and tariffs can also influence the fashion industry's sustainability efforts. Governments can incentivize the use of sustainable materials and ethical production practices by providing tax breaks or subsidies to brands that prioritize sustainability. Conversely, imposing tariffs on products that fail to meet environmental and social standards can discourage harmful practices and promote fair competition. By aligning trade policies with sustainability goals, governments can support the growth of responsible fashion brands and encourage industry-wide change.

Consumer protection laws play a crucial role in promoting transparency and accountability within the fashion industry. Regulations that require brands to disclose information about their supply chains, labor practices, and environmental impact empower consumers to make informed choices. Certification programs and eco-labels can provide additional assurance of a brand's commitment to sustainability. By fostering a culture of transparency and accountability, consumer protection laws can drive demand for ethical and sustainable fashion, encouraging brands to adopt responsible practices.

12

Chapter 12: The Intersection of Fashion and Climate Change

The fashion industry is a significant contributor to climate change, with its extensive use of resources and high levels of greenhouse gas emissions. From the production of raw materials to the transportation of finished garments, each stage of the fashion supply chain has an impact on the environment. Understanding the relationship between fashion and climate change is crucial for driving the industry toward more sustainable practices and mitigating its environmental footprint.

The production of textile fibers, particularly synthetic fibers like polyester, is energy-intensive and relies heavily on fossil fuels. The extraction and processing of petroleum to create synthetic fibers contribute to carbon emissions and environmental degradation. Additionally, the production of natural fibers such as cotton requires large amounts of water, pesticides, and fertilizers, further exacerbating the industry's environmental impact. By exploring alternative, eco-friendly materials and reducing reliance on resource-intensive processes, the fashion industry can play a vital role in addressing climate change.

The transportation and distribution of garments also contribute to the fashion industry's carbon footprint. Fast fashion's global supply chains involve the movement of raw materials and finished products across long distances, leading to significant greenhouse gas emissions. The reliance on air freight for rapid delivery further compounds the environmental impact. To mitigate these effects, fashion brands can adopt strategies such as localizing production, optimizing transportation routes, and exploring low-carbon logistics solutions. By rethinking supply chain logistics, the industry can reduce its carbon emissions and contribute to climate change mitigation.

Circular fashion practices offer a promising solution for reducing the fashion industry's impact on climate change. By promoting the reuse, recycling, and repurposing of garments, circular fashion reduces the need for new resource extraction and minimizes waste. This approach extends the lifecycle of clothing, reducing the demand for new products and conserving resources. Brands can implement circular economy principles by designing for longevity, offering take-back programs, and using recycled materials in their collections. By embracing circularity, the fashion industry can transition to a more sustainable model that aligns with climate action goals.

Consumer behavior also plays a crucial role in addressing the fashion industry's impact on climate change. By making conscious choices, such as reducing consumption, supporting sustainable brands, and prioritizing quality over quantity, consumers can drive demand for eco-friendly products. Additionally, adopting practices such as clothing swaps, secondhand shopping, and upcycling can help reduce the environmental footprint of fashion consumption. By fostering a culture of mindfulness and sustainability, consumers can contribute to the industry's efforts to combat climate change and promote a more sustainable future.

13

Chapter 13: The Role of Innovation in Sustainable Fashion

Innovation is at the heart of the sustainable fashion movement, driving the development of new materials, technologies, and business models that prioritize environmental and social responsibility. From biodegradable fabrics to digital fashion platforms, innovative solutions are transforming the fashion industry and paving the way for a more sustainable future.

One of the most exciting areas of innovation in sustainable fashion is the development of new materials that are both eco-friendly and versatile. Researchers and designers are exploring the potential of biodegradable and renewable materials, such as algae-based textiles, mushroom leather, and pineapple fibers. These materials offer sustainable alternatives to conventional textiles, reducing the industry's reliance on resource-intensive processes and minimizing environmental impact. The use of natural dyes and innovative dyeing techniques also contributes to the sustainability of fashion by reducing the use of harmful chemicals and conserving water.

Technology is playing a pivotal role in driving sustainability within the fashion industry. Digital fashion platforms and virtual try-ons are revolutionizing the way consumers engage with fashion, reducing the need for physical garments and minimizing waste. Augmented reality (AR) and virtual reality (VR) technologies allow consumers to visualize how garments will look and fit, enhancing the shopping experience and reducing the likelihood of returns. Additionally, AI-powered tools are helping brands optimize production processes, predict consumer preferences, and manage inventory more efficiently, reducing waste and overproduction.

The concept of "fashion as a service" is another innovative approach that promotes sustainability by rethinking traditional business models. Instead of owning garments, consumers can rent or lease clothing for a specified period, reducing the need for constant purchasing and minimizing waste. Subscription-based models and clothing rental services offer flexibility and variety, allowing consumers to enjoy fashion without the environmental impact of fast fashion. By embracing these new business models, the fashion industry can promote a more sustainable and circular economy.

Collaboration and partnerships are essential for driving innovation and sustainability within the fashion industry. By working together, brands, researchers, and organizations can share knowledge, resources, and best practices, accelerating the development of sustainable solutions. Initiatives such as industry coalitions, sustainability conferences, and innovation labs provide platforms for collaboration and innovation. By fostering a culture of collaboration, the fashion industry can overcome challenges and create a sustainable future that benefits both people and the planet.

14

Chapter 14: The Importance of Education and Awareness in Sustainable Fashion

Education and awareness are fundamental to the success of the sustainable fashion movement. By equipping consumers, designers, and industry professionals with the knowledge and skills to make informed decisions, education can drive positive change and promote a culture of sustainability within the fashion industry.

Consumer education plays a crucial role in raising awareness about the environmental and social impacts of fashion. Initiatives such as sustainability labels, certification programs, and educational campaigns provide valuable information about the origins, materials, and production methods of garments. By understanding the true cost of their clothing choices, consumers can make more conscious decisions that align with their values. Additionally, educational platforms and resources, such as documentaries, books, and online courses, offer insights into sustainable fashion practices and inspire consumers to adopt more mindful consumption habits.

Fashion education institutions also have a significant role to play in promoting sustainability within the industry. By incorporating sustainability, ethics, and social responsibility into fashion curricula, educational institutions can prepare the next generation of designers and industry professionals to create positive change. Workshops, internships, and collaborations with ethical brands provide students with hands-on experience in sustainable fashion practices, fostering a culture of innovation and social consciousness. By nurturing future leaders who prioritize sustainability, fashion education can drive the industry toward a more responsible and sustainable future.

Industry awareness and training are essential for promoting sustainable practices within fashion companies. By providing employees with the knowledge and tools to implement sustainable solutions, brands can integrate sustainability into their operations and decision-making processes. Training programs, workshops, and sustainability guidelines can help employees understand the environmental and social implications of their actions and encourage them to adopt more responsible practices. By fostering a culture of sustainability within organizations, the fashion industry can drive systemic change and promote environmental stewardship.

Advocacy and activism also play a crucial role in raising awareness and driving change within the fashion industry. Organizations, influencers, and activists are using their platforms to highlight the importance of sustainability and advocate for ethical practices. Campaigns such as Fashion Revolution and Sustainable Apparel Coalition raise awareness about the industry's impact and promote transparency and accountability. By engaging in advocacy and supporting organizations that champion sustainable fashion, individuals can contribute to the movement and drive positive change within the industry.

15

Chapter 15: The Role of Creativity and Innovation in Sustainable Fashion

Creativity and innovation are at the heart of the sustainable fashion movement. Designers, artists, and entrepreneurs are reimagining the fashion industry by developing new materials, technologies, and business models that prioritize environmental and social responsibility. From biodegradable fabrics to digital fashion platforms, innovative solutions are transforming the fashion industry and paving the way for a more sustainable future.

One of the most exciting areas of innovation in sustainable fashion is the development of new materials that are both eco-friendly and versatile. Researchers and designers are exploring the potential of biodegradable and renewable materials, such as algae-based textiles, mushroom leather, and pineapple fibers. These materials offer sustainable alternatives to conventional textiles, reducing the industry's reliance on resource-intensive processes and minimizing environmental impact. The use of natural dyes and innovative dyeing techniques also contributes to the sustainability of fashion by reducing the use of harmful chemicals and conserving water.

Technology is playing a pivotal role in driving sustainability within the fashion industry. Digital fashion platforms and virtual try-ons are revolutionizing the way consumers engage with fashion, reducing the need for physical garments and minimizing waste. Augmented reality (AR) and virtual reality (VR) technologies allow consumers to visualize how garments will look and fit, enhancing the shopping experience and reducing the likelihood of returns. Additionally, AI-powered tools are helping brands optimize production processes, predict consumer preferences, and manage inventory more efficiently, reducing waste and overproduction.

The concept of "fashion as a service" is another innovative approach that promotes sustainability by rethinking traditional business models. Instead of owning garments, consumers can rent or lease clothing for a specified period, reducing the need for constant purchasing and minimizing waste. Subscription-based models and clothing rental services offer flexibility and variety, allowing consumers to enjoy fashion without the environmental impact of fast fashion. By embracing these new business models, the fashion industry can promote a more sustainable and circular economy.

Collaboration and partnerships are essential for driving innovation and sustainability within the fashion industry. By working together, brands, researchers, and organizations can share knowledge, resources, and best practices, accelerating the development of sustainable solutions. Initiatives such as industry coalitions, sustainability conferences, and innovation labs provide platforms for collaboration and innovation. By fostering a culture of collaboration, the fashion industry can overcome challenges and create a sustainable future that benefits both people and the planet.

16

Chapter 16: The Intersection of Fashion and Technology

The fashion industry is experiencing a technological revolution that is transforming the way garments are designed, produced, and consumed. From smart textiles to digital fashion platforms, technology is driving innovation and sustainability in fashion. The integration of cutting-edge technologies is enabling brands to create more efficient and sustainable practices while enhancing the consumer experience.

Smart textiles, also known as e-textiles or electronic textiles, are revolutionizing the fashion industry by incorporating technology into fabrics. These textiles are embedded with sensors, conductive fibers, and other electronic components, allowing garments to interact with the wearer and the environment. Smart textiles have applications in various sectors, including health and wellness, sports, and fashion. For example, fitness apparel embedded with sensors can monitor vital signs and provide real-time feedback to the wearer. In fashion, smart textiles can be used to create garments that change color, texture, or shape in response to external stimuli, offering endless possibilities for creative expression.

Digital fashion platforms are transforming the way consumers engage with fashion by offering virtual experiences and reducing the need for physical garments. Virtual try-ons, powered by augmented reality (AR) and virtual reality (VR) technologies, allow consumers to visualize how garments will look and fit without trying them on in person. This technology enhances the shopping experience, reduces returns, and minimizes waste. Digital fashion also includes virtual garments and accessories that exist solely in the digital realm. Consumers can purchase and wear these virtual items in digital spaces, such as social media and gaming platforms, reducing the demand for physical clothing and promoting sustainable consumption.

3D printing technology is making waves in the fashion industry by enabling designers to create customized garments with minimal material waste. 3D printing allows for precise control over the amount of fabric used, reducing excess inventory and production waste. This technology also supports on-demand manufacturing, eliminating the need for mass production and overstocking. The ability to produce garments locally reduces the carbon footprint associated with transportation and logistics. 3D printing also offers new opportunities for creative expression, allowing designers to experiment with complex shapes, textures, and patterns that are difficult to achieve with traditional manufacturing methods.

Blockchain technology is enhancing transparency and traceability in the fashion supply chain. By providing a decentralized and tamper-proof ledger, blockchain enables brands to track the journey of a garment from raw material to finished product. This transparency ensures that ethical and sustainable practices are upheld at every stage of production. Consumers can access detailed information about the origins of their clothing, empowering them to make informed purchasing decisions. Blockchain also facilitates the authentication of products, reducing the prevalence of counterfeit goods in the market.

17

Chapter 17: The Collective Responsibility of Fashion

The journey toward a sustainable and ethical fashion industry requires collective responsibility and collaboration from all stakeholders. Brands, consumers, policymakers, and industry organizations must work together to create a future where fashion is synonymous with responsibility and sustainability. By embracing shared values and committing to positive change, we can transform the fashion industry into a force for good.

Fashion brands play a crucial role in driving sustainability by adopting ethical practices, eco-friendly materials, and transparent supply chains. By prioritizing sustainability in their business models, brands can reduce their environmental footprint and support the well-being of workers and communities. Innovations in sustainable design, production, and distribution offer opportunities for brands to lead the way in creating a more responsible fashion industry. By collaborating with suppliers, researchers, and organizations, brands can share knowledge and resources, accelerating the development of sustainable solutions.

Consumers also have a significant role to play in promoting sustainable fashion. By making conscious choices and supporting ethical brands, consumers can drive demand for eco-friendly products and encourage the industry to adopt more responsible practices. Mindful consumption, such as investing in quality over quantity, supporting secondhand and vintage clothing, and practicing clothing care and repair, can reduce waste and extend the lifespan of garments. By raising awareness and advocating for transparency and accountability, consumers can contribute to positive change within the fashion industry.

Policymakers and government agencies have the power to shape the fashion industry's approach to sustainability through regulations and incentives. By implementing policies that promote sustainable practices, limit the use of harmful chemicals, and encourage resource efficiency, governments can hold brands accountable for their environmental and social impacts. Extended Producer Responsibility (EPR) schemes, trade policies, and consumer protection laws can drive the industry toward a more sustainable and equitable future. By collaborating with industry stakeholders, policymakers can create a regulatory framework that supports ethical practices and environmental stewardship.

Industry organizations and advocacy groups play a vital role in driving awareness and promoting best practices within the fashion industry. By organizing initiatives, campaigns, and conferences, these organizations provide platforms for collaboration and knowledge-sharing. Certifications and eco-labels offer valuable information about a brand's commitment to sustainability, empowering consumers to make informed choices. Advocacy groups raise awareness about the environmental and social impacts of fashion, advocating for transparency, accountability, and positive change. By supporting these organizations and engaging in advocacy, individuals can contribute to the movement for sustainable fashion.

The Fabric of Responsibility: Ecology, Ethics, and the Future of Fashion

In a world where fashion trends change at lightning speed, "The Fabric of Responsibility" delves into the intricate relationship between fashion, ecology, and ethics. This thought-provoking book explores the hidden environmental and social costs of the fashion industry, from the depletion of natural resources to exploitative labor practices. Through 17 meticulously crafted

CHAPTER 17: THE COLLECTIVE RESPONSIBILITY OF FASHION

chapters, the book unravels the threads of fast fashion, the environmental impact of textile production, and the importance of ethical sourcing and fair trade.

As the narrative unfolds, readers are introduced to innovative technologies and sustainable practices reshaping the industry. From smart textiles to regenerative agriculture, the book highlights the potential of technology and creativity in driving positive change. It also emphasizes the power of consumer choice and the role of education and awareness in fostering a culture of sustainability.

"The Fabric of Responsibility" challenges readers to rethink their relationship with fashion, advocating for a future where style and ethics coexist harmoniously. By embracing shared values and collective responsibility, we can transform the fashion industry into a force for good, ensuring a thriving future for both people and the planet.

www.ingramcontent.com/pod-product-compliance
Lightning Source LLC
LaVergne TN
LVHW020458080526
838202LV00057B/6034